D0000905
nakaba suzuki presents
22
The Demons didn't see that one coming!
It looks like the Festival ends here.
How fitting that "Pride" should be Sir Escanor, the strongest Holy Knight.
ZSH
ZSH
RRRRUMBLE
He has magnificent judgment and ability that clears the way before him.
I've heard this man's voice somewhere before.
And something about his magic feels familiar.
Who is he...?

CONTENTS

Chapter 171 - The Time Has Come

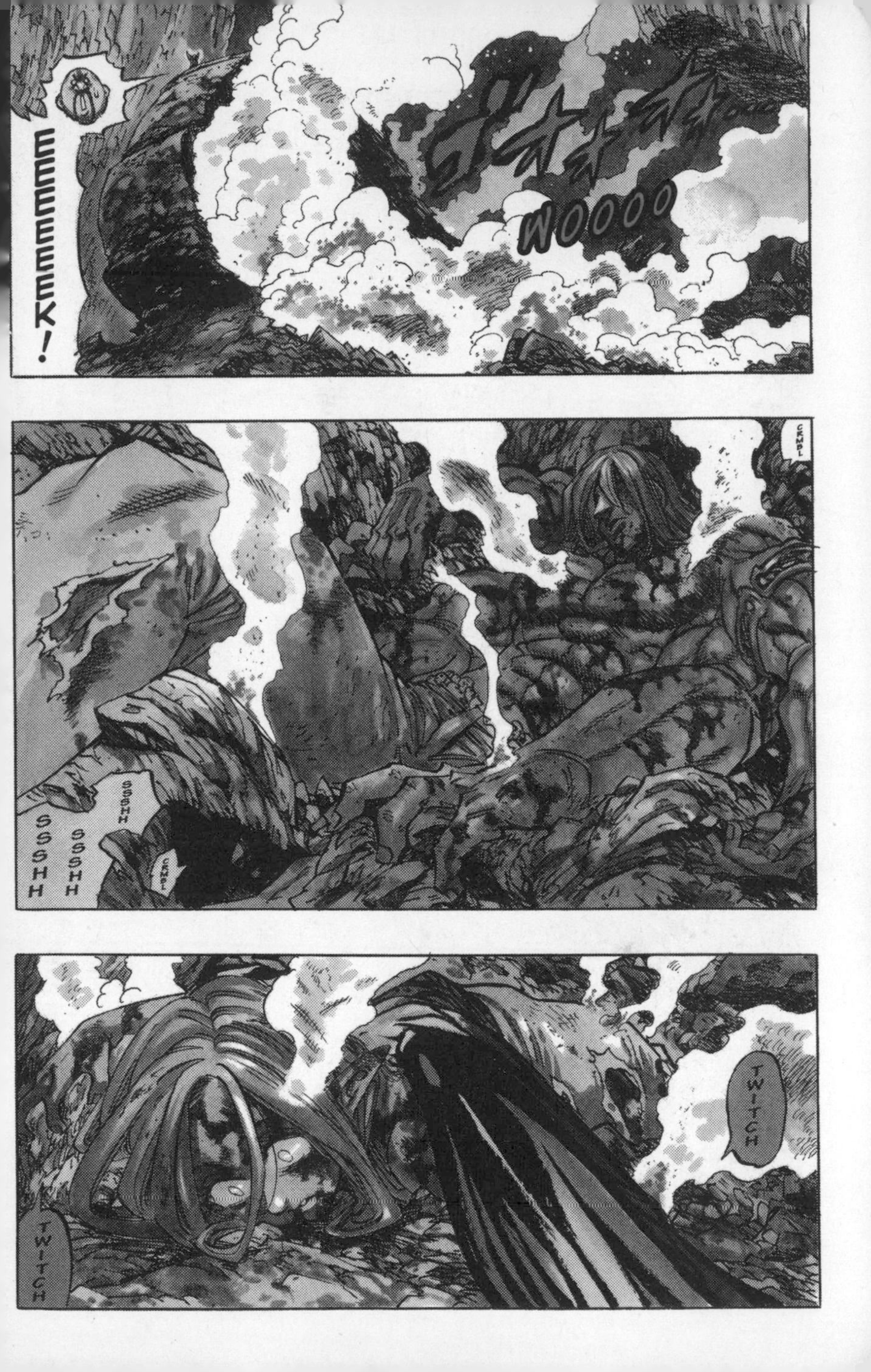
WOOOO
EEEEEEEK!
CRMBL
SSSHH
SSSHH
SSSHH
CRMBL
TWITCH
TWITCH

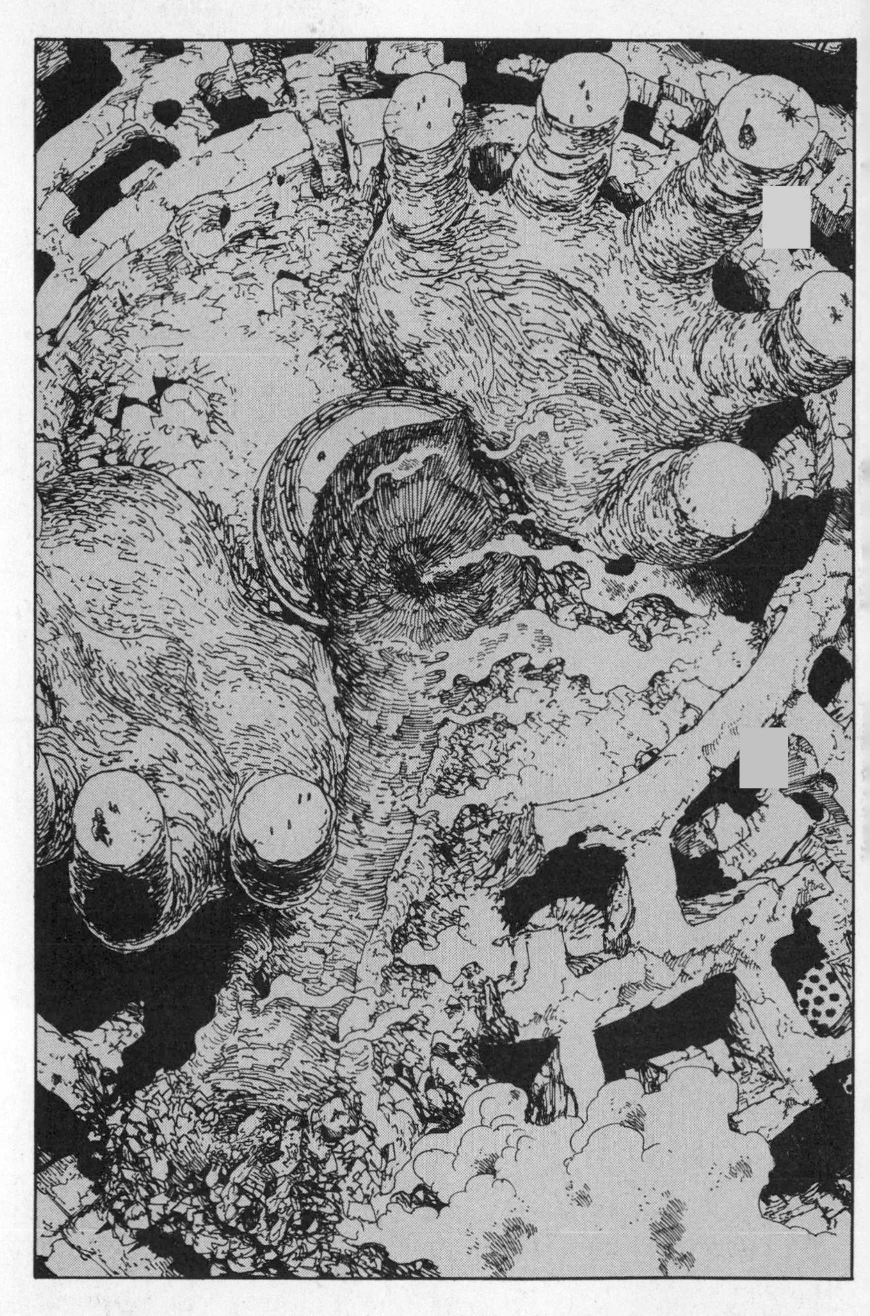

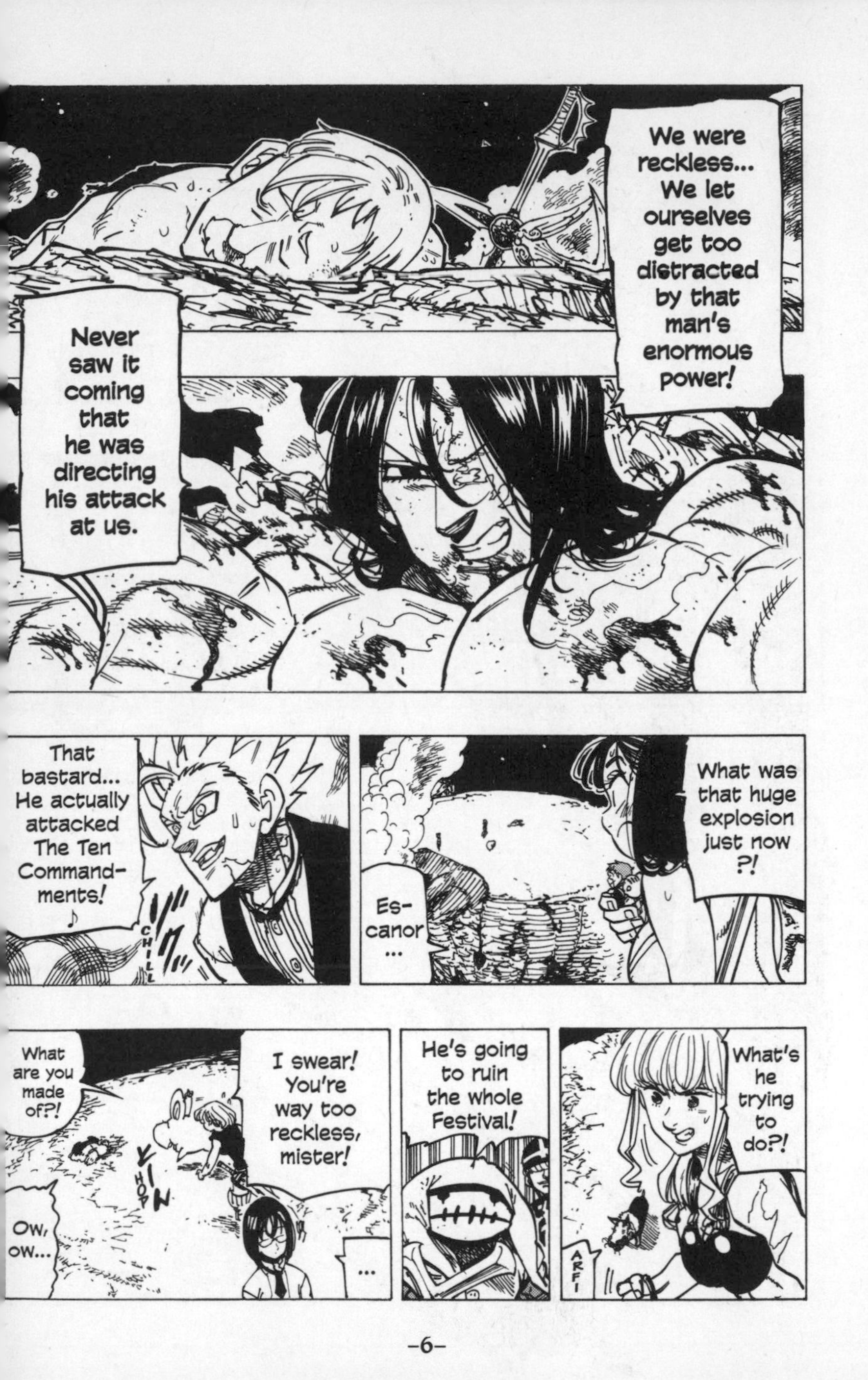
We were reckless... We let ourselves get too distracted by that man's enormous power!
Never saw it coming that he was directing his attack at us.
What was that huge explosion just now?!
Es-canor...
That bastard... He actually attacked The Ten Command-ments! ♪
CHILL
What's he trying to do?!
ARF!
He's going to ruin the whole Festival!
I swear! You're way too reckless, mister!
...
What are you made of?!
HOP
Ow, ow...

WHIP
CAP'N, WHAT DO WE—
!!
BOOM

CRMBL
Let's get to this Festival's main event.
CRMBL
CRMBL
CRMBL

!!!!
WHOOM
SWSH

HMPH!
WHOOSH

BAM
WHOOSH
LURCH

HAAH...!
WHACK
WHACK
WHACK

REEL
CLENCH
HOP
HOP
HOP
HOP
KAPOW

CHILL CHILL
ZZING

THUD
THUD
CHINK

You had that all planned out.
LICK

I was waiting for this moment.
For my chance to land a sure strike on the two of you!

Melio-das... is scaring me.
He was waiting for a chance to strike?!
I didn't hear anything about that strategy!
UN-BELIEVABLE THEY'RE ALL MONSTERS
I knew that if I came for you head-on all by myself, the two of you would be on your guard and ready for me. Even I'd fail in a fight like that.
So, in order to catch you off guard, I came as a participant with my friends to enjoy the Festival.

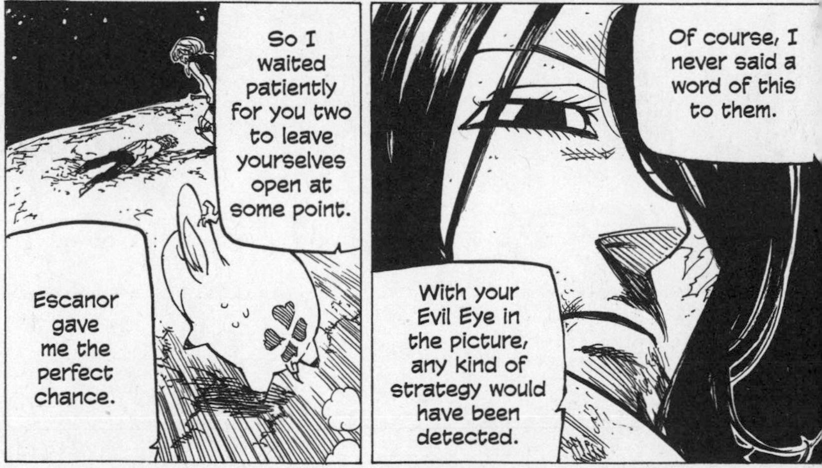
Of course, I never said a word of this to them.
With your Evil Eye in the picture, any kind of strategy would have been detected.
So I waited patiently for you two to leave yourselves open at some point.
Escanor gave me the perfect chance.

KOFF!
PUSH
CATCH
WHY DID YOU DO SUCH A THING?
Gowther-kun... even if you...don't have a heart... you're still... one of The Seven... Deadly Sins.
I couldn't... forgive those Command-ments...for toying...with my friend's... emotions.
WHAT YOU ARE SAYING IS A CONTRADICTION. I CANNOT HAVE EMOTIONS IF I HAVE NO HEART.
Ha... Ha ha...Are you...really sure about... that?
GLOOOW
POP

I see...
It's true, there's no doubt that in a one-on-one battle we'd be forced into a tight match.
"GIGANT EMBRACE."
EEEEK!
What's going on?!
RRRRRRRUMBLE
But you made a fatal mistake.

FWIP
SLAM
FLING
EEE-
EEE-
EK!
UWAA-
AAA-
AH!

ドポン
POOMF
NOW I HAVE EVERY-ONE IN MY CLUTCHES.
IF YOU OPPOSE ME, I'LL KILL THEM ALL.

BOOOM

I'll kill you first.
BASH

SNAP
KA-BOOM
I must say, that was a close one. That almost sent me packing to the afterlife.
I'll restore you in no time, so just hold tight, Drole-kun.
SPIRIT SPEAR BASQUIAS, FIFTH FORM
"YGGDRASIL ARMOR!"

We're going to turn this match right around between the two of us.
PSSHT
FLINK
CRACK
POP
!!
OMP
GIVE IT UP.
ZAP

ZAP

YOU GUYS DON'T HAVE A CHANCE.
ZAP
BOAR HAT

Bonus Story - "On the Road to Vaizel" (1)

To Be Continued on Page 48

Chapter 172 - To You Who Were Once My Friend

Three beings who once fought together to bring down the Demon Lord are now enemies... Fate really is ironic.

RMBL
Meliodas, I want to hear how you really feel.
You don't actually want a fight to the death, do you?
ZSH

Of course I do.
I know both the reasons and feelings behind why you two turned over to the other side.
ZSH

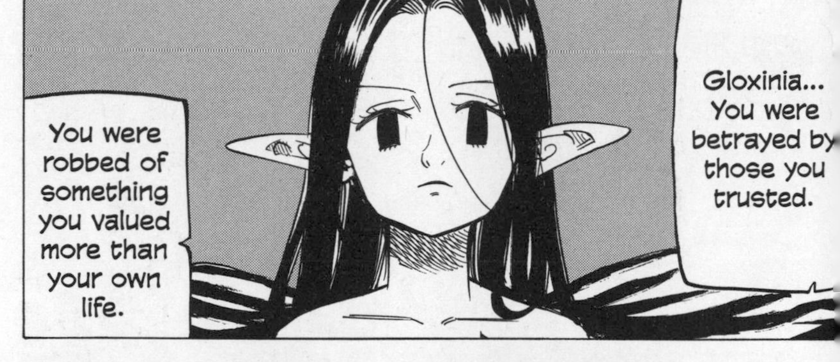
Gloxinia... You were betrayed by those you trusted.
You were robbed of something you valued more than your own life.

Drole... You were a warrior who always aimed to be the strongest.
But that pride of yours was trampled and crushed underfoot.

If you know us so well, then why—
ZSH
But.

The moment you went to the dark side, it was over!

LUNGE

SPIRIT SPEAR BASQUIAS, FIRST FORM "BASQUIAS."

Too bad ...

GLOW

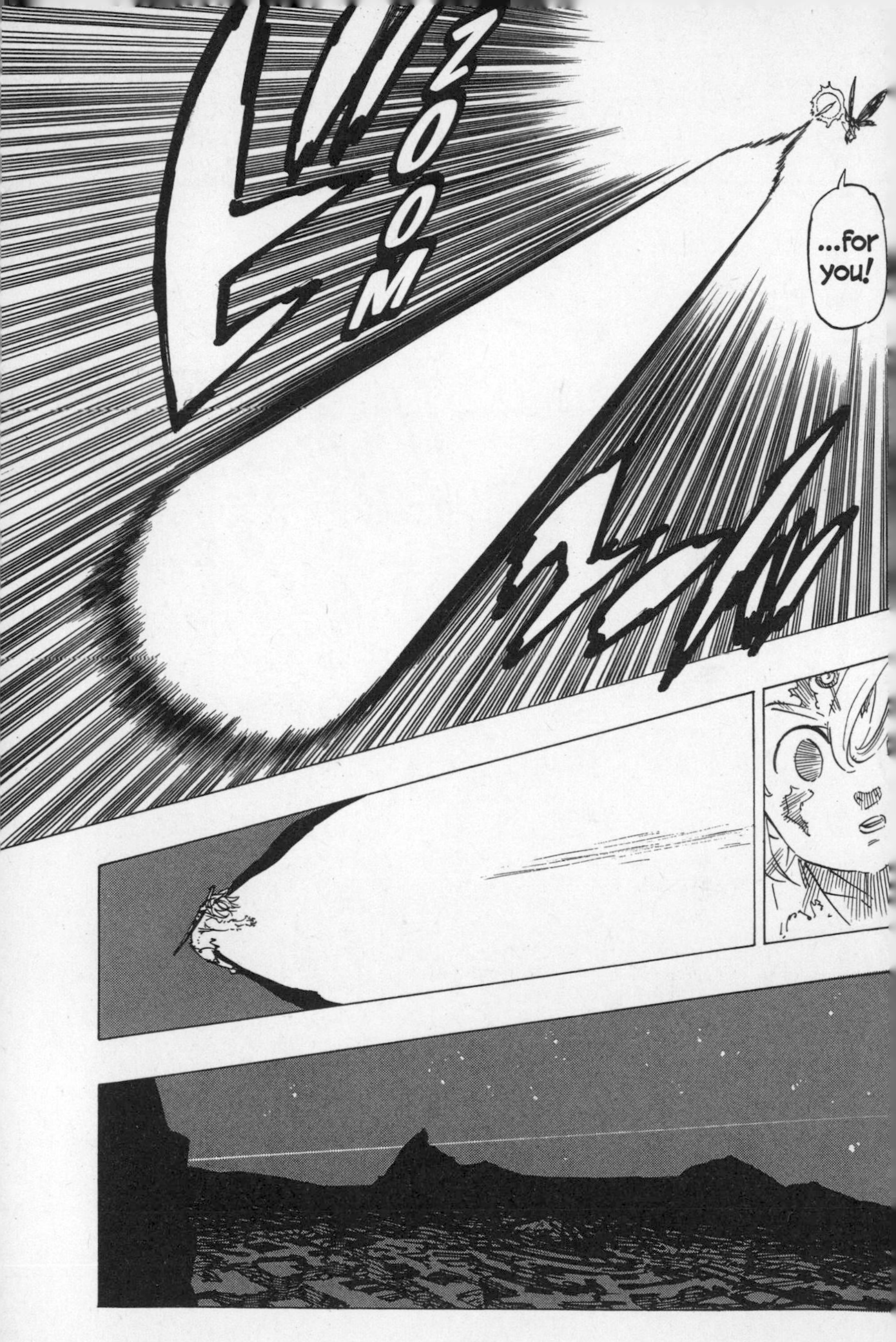
ZOOM
...for you!

FLASH
THOOOOOM
WHAT A MONUMENTAL CLASH OF ENERGY.
Melio-das-sama!
He's being too rash, thinking he can take on those monsters all on his own!
Come on, guys! Let's go give Meliodas some backup!
What good will going to him do?
SNOINK?!

THOOM
How many seconds would you last out there on that field?
All you'll do is trip the Cap'n up.
But that's ...!
Ban's right.

His opponents are The Ten Commandments. They possess powers on a whole other dimension from what we've faced so far.

In short... Only Meliodas is a match for them, given the situation. We're not abandoning him.

But isn't our being trapped here a handicap for him?
CLANG
This bedrock is impenetrable!
Even if we wanted to escape, there's no breaking it.
How're we supposed to get out of here?

Let me handle it.
JANGLE
I will teleport all of us here to a safe location.
Gilfrost, was it? You can move this huge crowd in one go?
It's so cramped in here.
Well, I'll do what I can.
Don't even joke like that! I'm staying right here. I'm not about to withdraw from this Festival!
No! We have to get away while we still can!
But then Zol and Della—
I've got an idea! Okay, Matrona?
There's no time. Here goes!

"DROP OF LIFE."
SPIRIT SPEAR BASQUIAS, SEVENTH FORM "MOON ROSE."
Now to restore you.
KABOOM
SWISH
SWF
SWF
Just wait two or three seconds.

ZLOOSH
"CURSED VINE TREE."
WOOD
Sorry, but I can't wait.
VOOM
SLASH
SLASH
SLASH
SLASH

SLICE
SLAM
HAH !!

Kah ...
CRUNCH
ZIP
Farewell, comrade.
"GIGA CRUSH"!!

THOOM
THOOM
THOOM
THOOM
THOOM

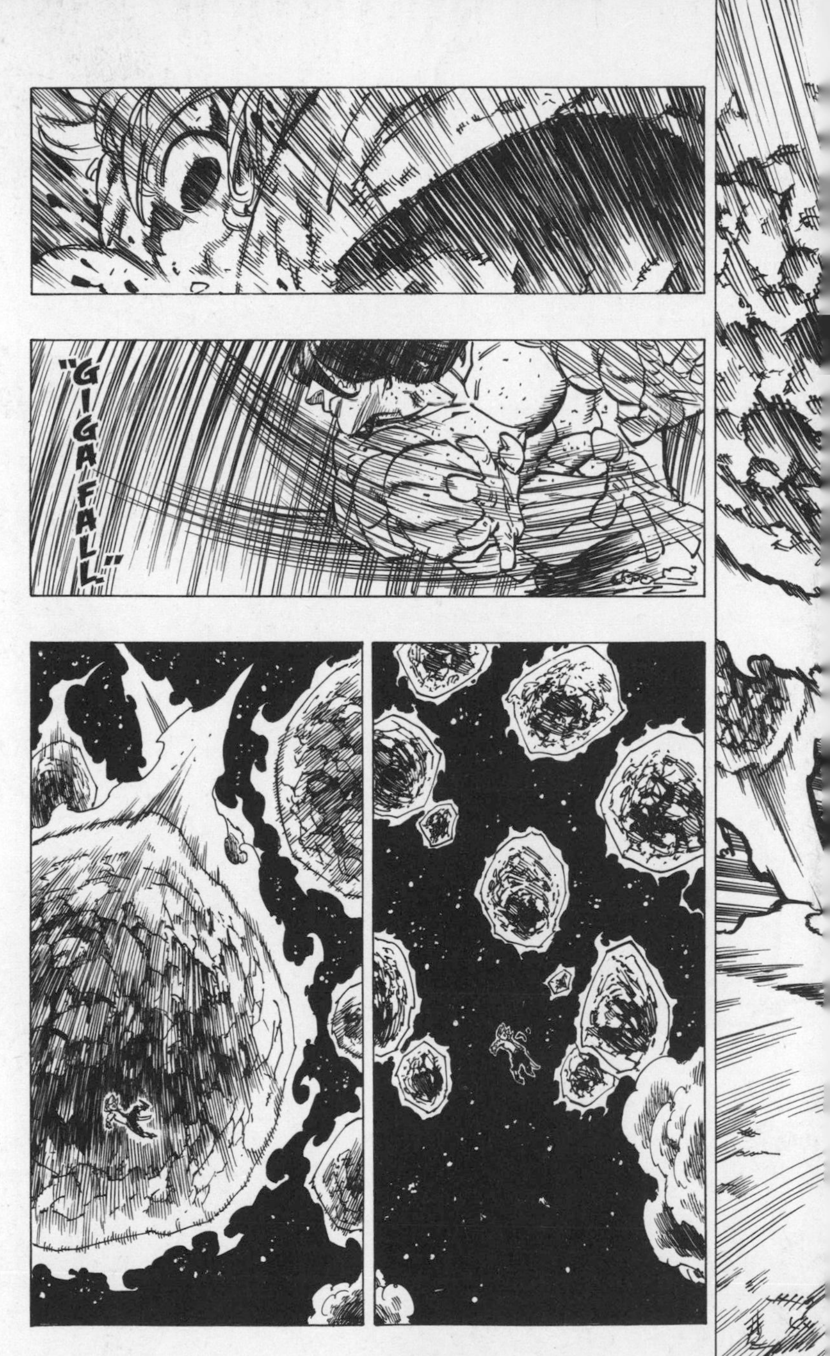
"GIGA FALL"

RRRRUMBLE

...?
Is... Is this Liones Castle?
Ooh! Th... That was awesome!
HAAH! HAAH! HAAH!

RRRUMBLE
W...Wa
don't t
me thi
is...
AFTERSHOCKS FROM THE FIGHT IN VAIZEL ARE REACHING US HERE.
The Ten Command-ments should have neve been al-lowed to awaken!
SWF
It would be no exaggeration to say that they are walking natural disasters!
...
But... what about Meliodas-sama ?!
That is why I cannot quell this trepidation.
Huh ?

For Meliodas shall triumph.

Bonus Story - "On the Road to Vaizel" (2)

THE END

Chapter 173 - The Darkness Comes Down

SLASH
BOOM
....!
"GOD RIPPER!"

WOOOSH
ZSH
"HEAVY METAL"
Nice... one!
TIIING

SPIRIT SPEAR BASQUIAS, SEVENTH FORM "MOON ROSE."
"DROP OF LIFE."
FZZZT
SSHHH
SWF
KOFF... HAAH!!
ZIP
ZOOSH
"DROP OF LIFE."

Whoa!
ZIP
FWIP
SWISH
TING
TING
TING
TING
TCHI

BASH
"GIGA PICK"!!
GRAB
WHIP
WHIP
WHIP
HOP

SMACK
THOOM
スタッ
TMP

The Captain...is incredible!
He's holding his own and then some...
...against two of the legendary Ten Com-mandments!

MORE ACCURATELY SPEAKING, HE'S ALTERNATING RENDERING ONE OR THE OTHER INCAPABLE O FIGHTING, SO AS TO KEEP IT CONSTANTL ONE-TO-ONE.
OF COURSE, CONSIDER-ING THE CAPTAIN'S LEVEL OF STRENGTH, IT'S THE MOST PLAUSIBLE FEAT TO PERFORM.
...

Gowther's right... Just with his original strength restored, Meliodas can fight plenty well enough, and he's enveloped in that Demon power. He should be overwhelming!
To be honest, it looks to me like he's doing sloppy work and cutting corners.

Either way, it's clear Meliodas knows these Ten Command-ments guys.
That one Com-mand-ment said it himself ♪
He called the Cap'n a back-stabber of the Demon race.

But... whether he's a Demon or not...
...the Cap'n's still the Cap'n.

I don't really follow, but...
!!
...Meliodas is a nice guy. I don't think he has an ulterior motive.
Just like you, Harle-quin.
ドキッ
THADUMP

Diane ...
THE ENEMY OF OUR ENEMY IS OUR FRIEND!
ジロ…
GLARE
For your information, I still haven't forgiven you.

Meliodas-sama, please come back safe no matter what!
ゴゴゴゴ…
RRRRUMBLE

Melio...das... you're as strong and sentimental as ever.
Why... would you side with... those pathetic Humans? There's no saving them.
If you wanted... you could even claim the throne of the Demon Lord.
I can see it now. You cannot fight unemotionally, and it'll lead you to miserable defeat.
CRMBL
I had no idea your suffering warped you guys so badly.
CHING

In that case, I'll end...
...your suffering for you!
GLEAM

BOOM
BOOM
BOOM
BOOM
BOOM
BOOM
BWAH
CRACK
CRACK
RACK
CRMBL
Melio-das-sama... Melio-das-sama?!
What appened?! Suddenly hese things came out of the sky from every direction.

FLINCH
Wh... What's this magic energy?
HE EMITTE TOO MUCH BLOODLUS DURING THIS FIGHT
This...
This is the worst thing that could happen!
Cap'n ...
GET OUT OF THERE!!

ZSH

Chapter 174 - Meliodas vs. The Ten Commandments

RRRRUMBLE
He's surrounded... by The Ten Commandments!
H... Hey, Gil! That's...
...Chief Holy Knight Dreyfus?!
Father ...
He's the one who spearheaded the destruction our homeland, Malaxia!
What's he planning this time with those monsters?! Answer me, Hendrickson!

Huh? But they're short one. If I remembe correctly, his name was Galland...
Yeah, if you're looking for him, this fellow here... Escanor crushed him.
Huh ?!
N...Nice to meet you.
RIGHT ?
But... Damn it! Melascula... That woman's still alive.
Ban... That's why I'm still...
Elaine ...
Please! Teleport Meliodas-sama here to us!
I can't! I would have to go there and retrieve him myself. The Ten Commandments would never give me the chance...!
...!!
ZSH

SLASH

チン…
CHNK

BASH
ZSSSH
YANK

STOMP
DO IT.

LACK CLACK CLACK
"BINDING RESENTMENT."
What was that just now? An attack spell?
I don't know... But it's outrageously powerful magic!
S-SLIDE
...?
SSSHHH

POW
POW
POW
ZLOOSH
BASH
SNAP

FLIP
What'd he do?!
A smoke screen!
POOOOM
?!!
POOF

All right! He got ou of The Te Command ments' circle!
HOP
FZZT
FZZT
THIS... IS WHAT "BINDING RESENT-MENT" DOES.
YOU HAVE BEEN CURSED ...
...SO THAT YOU CANNOT LEAVE THIS PLACE.
DEATH IS ALL THAT AWAITS YOU NOW.

A...Are you kidding me?! So he can't escape? That means Meliodas will either defeat The Ten Commandments or be defeated by them...
Don't talk like that, Hawk-chan!
SNOINK!
I...
I AN'T ELP IT!
SMACK
CLANG
BAM

WHACK
BASH BASH BASH
ZIP
S... Something's off about this.
She's getting stronger and stronger!
T-THUD
?!
KERTHUD
...!!
KAPOW
Don't tell me you've forgotten Derieri's "Combo Star."
TWIST TWIST
It's a super offensive specialized magic that, as long as her combination attacks hit their mark without any break, adds 200,000 pounds of weight with each strike.

BASH
WHAM
THUD
CRASH
BAM

53
...
FZZT
WHOOSH
54
!!
BOOM

GRAB
Impressive. You're the second person to withstand over 50 of Derieri's "Combo Star" strikes.
TOSS
Now with both your arms crushed, you're not capable of "Full Counter."
ZOOOOOM
"HELL'S PHOE-NIX."

STOP
IIIIIT
!!
FWOOSH

KA-BOOM
SLASH

TMP
BOOOM
Not bad.
GASH
STRAAAIN
PLOP
I gotta be frank with you, that was so lame.
I'm... I'm not even going to translate that.

R
R
R
R
R
RUMBLE

Chapter 175 - To My Beloved Meliodas

TELEPORT ME TO MELIODAS THIS INSTANT!
Even if I did, you'd only die in vain!
I DON'T CARE!
DROP
Whoa, whoa!
Hup!
CATCH
I... can't!
GRAB
I can't have you dying on me!
FWAP
You're ...
That ring...

Hey, Matrona. You really think that those monsters... no matter how amazingly strong they are...
...would save Zol and Della ?!
...
ZSH
ZSH
You look even more worn out by your fight with Gloxinia and Drole than I'd thought.
ZSH

You have no idea how eagerly I've awaited this day.
I haven't forgotten the humiliation I suffered from being defeated in Danafall. However, by not destroying me then, you have sealed your fate now.
ZSH

I guess Dreyfus and Hendrickson didn't mess up your life enough.
What's he talking about?
What's Dreyfus saying?
You certainly are a sinful man.
CLANG
...

Dreyfus...! You're a strong-willed man! Don't let this piece of shit get the better of you!
Wake up!
Chase him out from within and get out of here!
No matte how you may try appealing to his heart, it' futile.
You'll never reach—
...Drey...
...fus...
FADE
Meliodas ...?!
STREAM

"MILKY WAY..."
"...JAIL BREAK BLADE" !!
ZWOOSH

No...
MELIO
DAS!
NO!
Stop... Stop it.
Drey-
fus!
Ha
ha ha!
That's not my father!
Gria-
more...

This is what you get for siding with the Humans!
ZWIP
Glox-inia-sama ...
... lease on't.
SPIRIT SPEAR BASQUIAS. FIRST FORM
"BASQUIAS."
RRRRRRUMBLE

FLASH
TRMBL
TRMBL
Melio-das!

CRMBL
CLATTER
FLAKE
FLAKE
Ah...
Ah...
It can't be...
Can it...?
Cap'n...

Brother Melio-das.
With your death, part one of our revenge is complete.

If not for you, we would have never suffered such humiliation.
It was your betrayal that made us Demons the losers in the war.

ニヤリ
GRIN
TAK

WHOOSH

D...Don't tell me... This is like what happened before!
CAP'N ?!
IT APPEARS HE WAS MERELY PRETEND-ING TO BE OVER-WHELMED BY THEM.
HE MUST HAVE ELECTED TO MAKE THAT FEINT AS THE ONLY FEASIBLE WAY OF DEFEATING THEM ALL.

THE AMOUNT OF MAGIC ACCUMULATED DURING THE DECISIVE BATTLE AT THE CAPITAL IS NO COMPARISON TO THE MAGIC HE'S GATHERED NOW.

I CALCU-LATE ITS FORCE ALONE TO BE APPROXI-MATELY 30 TIMES AS GREAT.

This is bad
You little ...
Will we once again be defeated by you?!

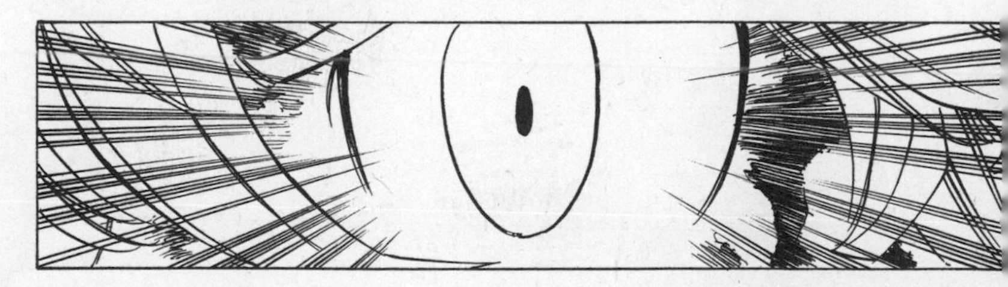

"REVENGE COUNTER!!!"

グアァァァァァァ
WOOOOOOOO

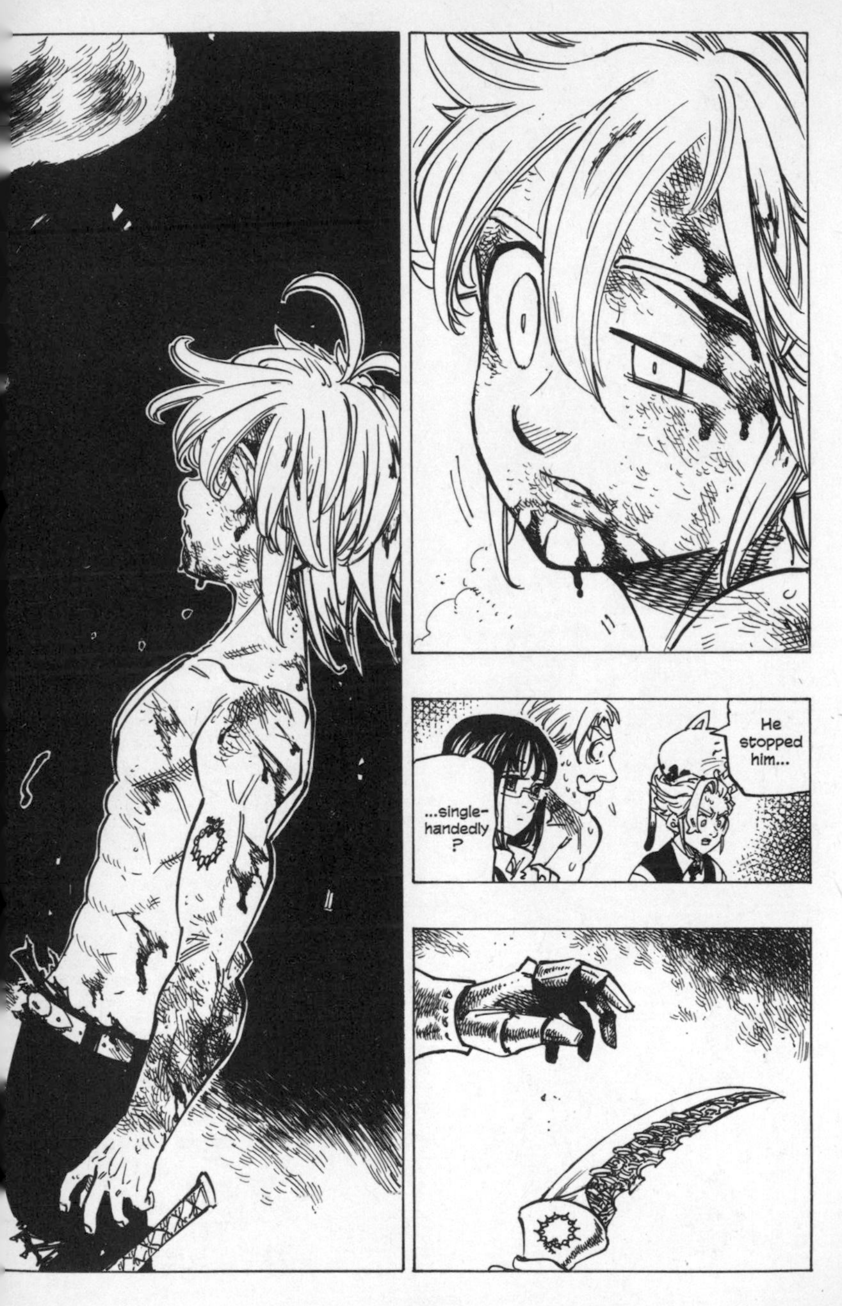
He stopped him...
...single-handedly?

Listen, Meliodas
I really wish I didn't have to do this.
TAP
Don't you see?
THUD
CLACK
GRIND
GRIND

IT'S BE-CAUSE I LOVE YOU.
AAAH...GAAAAAAH...AAAAAAAAH!
CRACK
SNAP

Chapter 176 - The Darkness Speaks

CRACK
CRACK
This brings back memories, Meliodas.
Let me hear your voice again.
GUH...AAAAAAAH!!
For a moment there, I was scared about how things might turn out. But I knew we could count on you, Estarossa.
SNAP
CRACK
AAH... GAH! AAA-AAH!!
Glad you're here, Gloxinia. Think you could heal my wounds?
Sure, but...
...it'll mean I'll be all out of "Drop of Life."

SPIRIT SPEAR BASQUIAS, SEVENTH FORM "MOON ROSE." "DROP OF LIFE."
SSSHHH
Hah!
AAAH...!
AAAAAAAAAAH
HAAAH!♡
GLOW
PERK
SNAP
GWAAH!

Hey, Esta-rossa. I gotta be frank with you.
You sure about this?
SNAP
GAH...AAAUGH!!
"I've been having the oddest sensation that we're being watched. It's likely Meliodas's friends. Should we be letting them free like this?" Is that what you mean?
Mm-hm.
Th-Th... They're on to us!!
SNOINK
THE SEVEN DEADLY SINS...
MELIO-DAS'S NEW... FRIENDS.
ZSH
New friends... indeed.

When were yo planning to betray them this time?
Like when you, The Ten Command-ments' commander, abandoned us...
GRAB

Your strength... and cold-heartedness back then was tremendous.
Those impotent Goddesses kept their distance out of fear of you.
Anybody could see that you were fit to be the next Demon Lord.

SLASH
I idolized you.

But then you suddenly turned your back on us, wrought havoc on the Demon world, and disappeared.
HAH—
CHOKE
FLAKE
FLAKE
Murdering two of The Ten Com-mandments on the way.

Drole and Gloxinia.
Until they joined later, there were two vacant seats in The Ten Com-mandments.

The balance that had been maintained between the Demons and the Goddesses crumbled magnificently.
Seeing it as their chance, the Goddesses called upon the other races to crush the Demons in one go.

You started the war 3,000 years ago.
Tell me.
What did it take for you to think up such a fun thing to do?
So the one who caused the bloody war in Britannia that involved all five races 3,000 years ago was...
SHOCK
...THE CAP-TAIN?

So this time you're substituting The Seven Deadly Sins for The Ten Command-ments.
I bet that, deep down, you can't wait until you get to betray them again.

ZSSSH
You really are a villain.

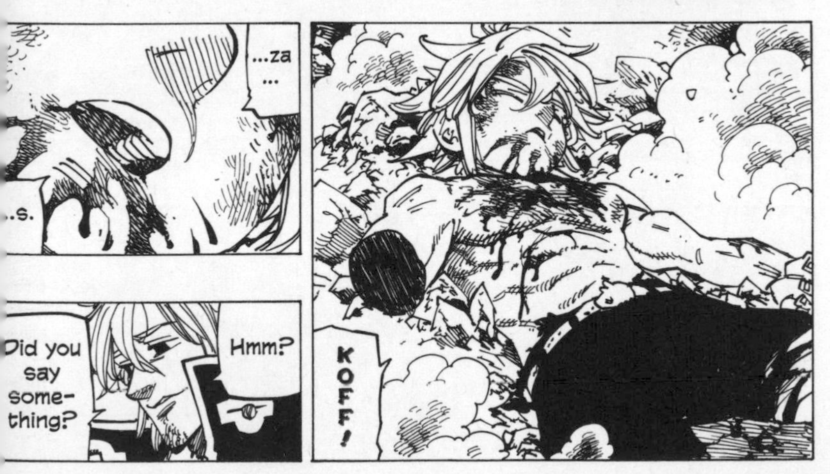
...za ...
...s.
KOFF!
Hmm?
Did you say some-thing?

Let me deliver the final blow against Meliodas.
SSFFFF
...
You? Why?
His little friends put me through hell.
Don't you think it's only natural Meliodas should be held responsible for their mischief?

Uh-oh..
She's going to take his so...
BAN!
WHIP
B... Ban?!
WAAAH!

You don't have to ask for my permission.
Thanks.
GLINT
Hey, you magician. ♪
...?

ZSH
ZSH
TWITCH
UH...
GUH...
ZSSSH
Oh, my... You're resisting.
But I am a master at manipulating the dead... and souls.
ZSSSH
GUH...
It'll be a piece of cake extracting your soul. You can't even move.
FLICK
THADUMP

SLIP
"SUMMON SOUL."
At that mo-ment ...
...The Ten Command-ments had no idea there was an intruder among them.

I might lose you again.
But I swear I'll bring you back to life someday, so...
It's okay, Ban. Save him...

"ZERO SIGN."
You don't have to ask for my permission.

Meliodas, I wonder what your soul tastes...
...LIGKHE?!
CRUNCH

WHO... 'RE YOU?
GAA-BBAH... GUHFF!
I can't under-stand what you're saying. ♫
ゴキッ
CRACK
?!!
"FOX HUNT."

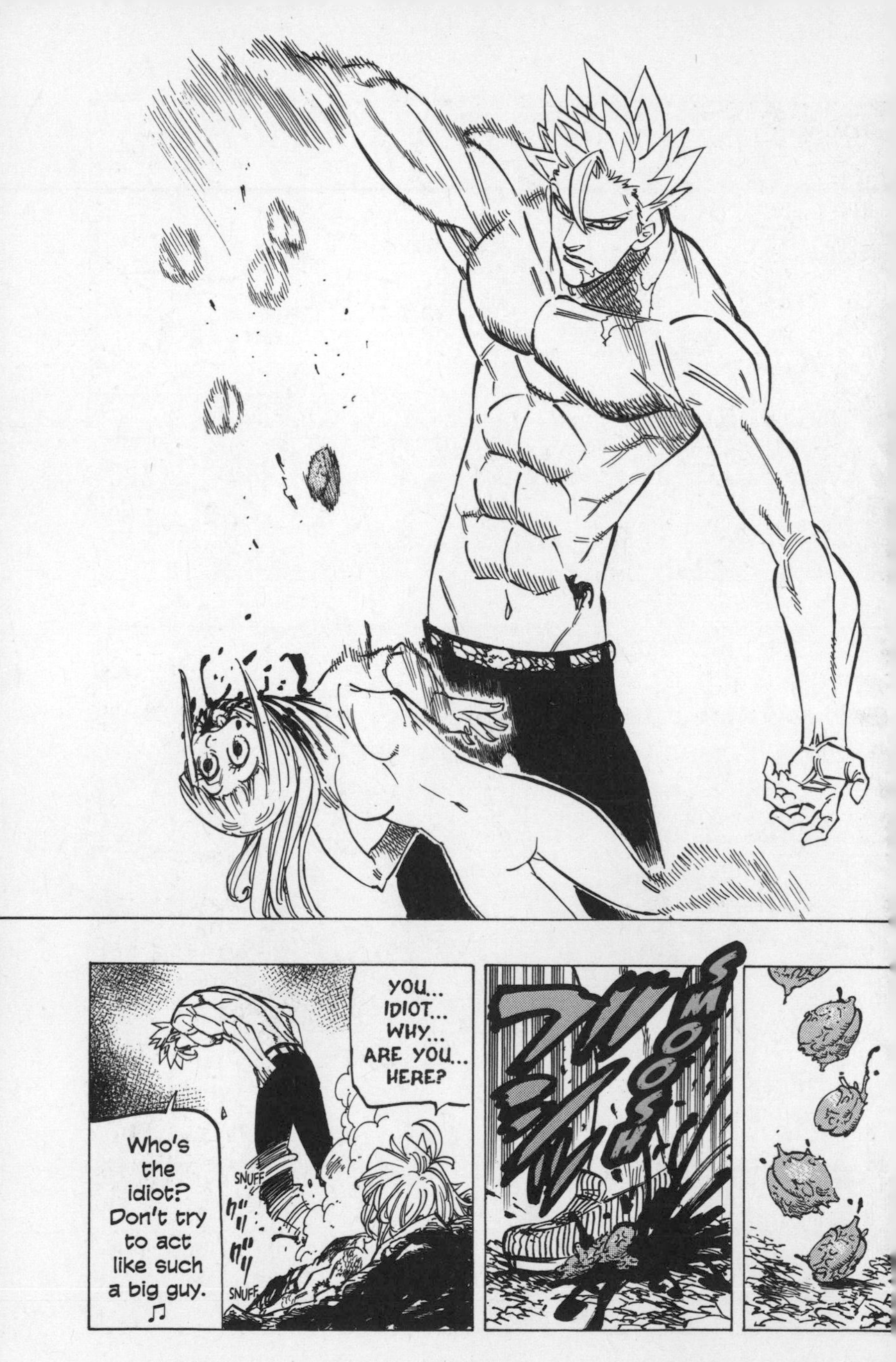
SMOOSH
YOU... IDIOT... WHY... ARE YOU... HERE?
Who's the idiot? Don't try to act like such a big guy. ♫
SNUFF
SNUFF

YOU'RE THE... BIGGEST IDIOT THERE IS!
Yeah, well. ♫
Like they say, idiots get along best. ♫

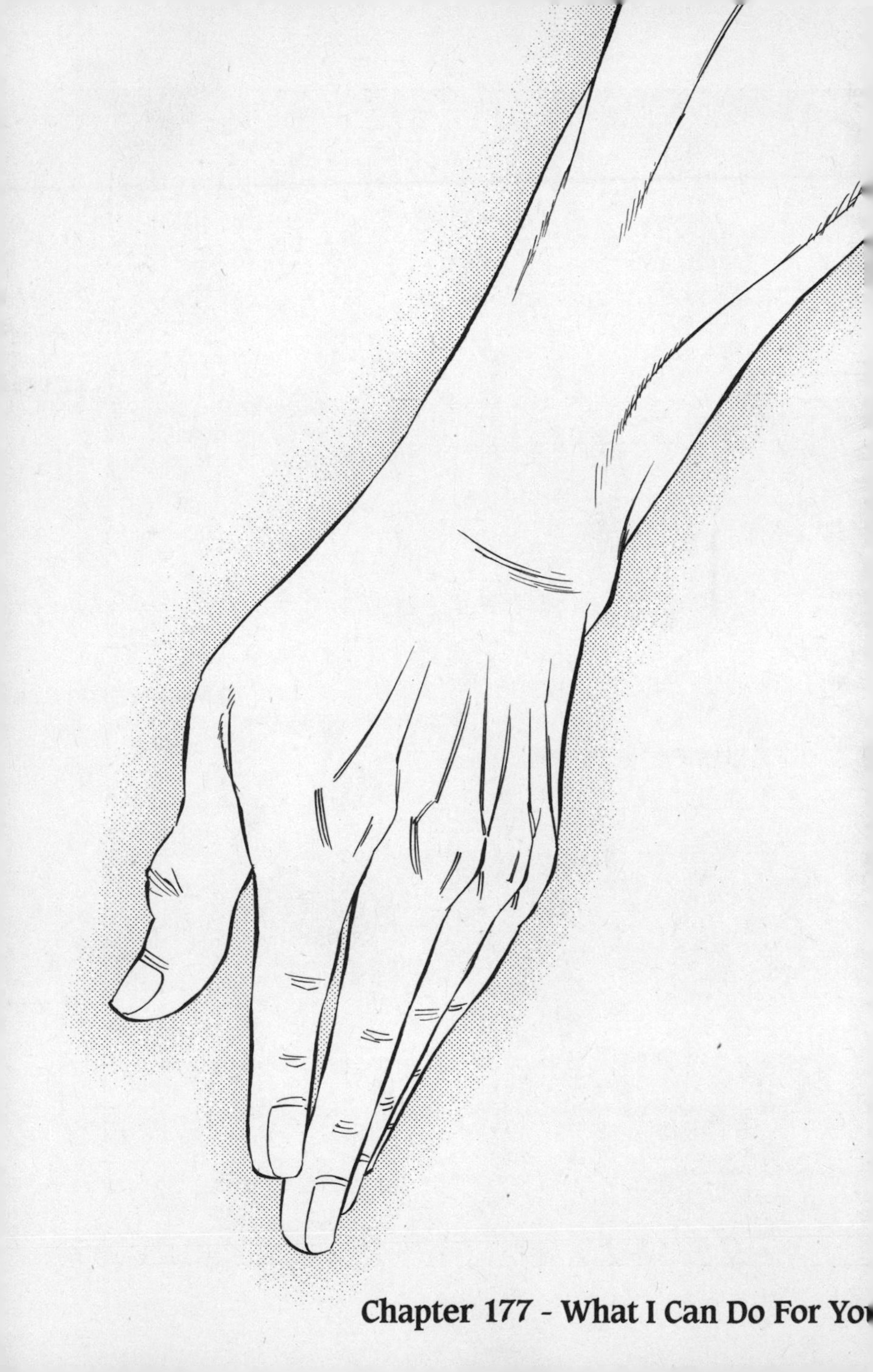

Chapter 177 - What I Can Do For You

YOU IDIOT.
DO I LOOK... HURT TO YOU?
YANK
GRIP
Can you stand up, Cap'n? ♪
That's The Seven Deadly Sins!...
Ban!
MELA-SCULA!!

She tried to eat my brother's soul without even asking.
She had death coming to her.
Human. You have my thanks.
If you hadn't gotten to her first, I would've killed her myself.
ZSH
Cap'n... get back.

ZSH
Meliodas must die at my hands.
THADUMP
KAH ...
GAH!

Cap-
By the way, what did you come here for?
THUD
WHAT DO YOU THINK ?!
"REBELLION!!"

ZIP
"FOX HUNT."
...!!
BSSHT
TAP
I'm going to teach you some-thing.
We high-ranking Demons have seven hearts.

STAB
This gets ric of the second one.
GWAH ...
Any Demon will die if all of their hearts are destroyed.
GRAB

STRAAAAIN
Not if I can help it!
STAB
3.
!!
"HUNTER FEST"!!
STAB
4.
5.
STAB

I WON'T LET YOU KILL THE CAP'N !!
GAAAAAH!
CRICK
STAB
I can't protect my woman ...
...or my one friend in the world?!
6.

STOP... IT...
GOODBYE, BROTHER. MY BELOVED MELIODAS.

STAB

AAAAAH!
I must say... you've been annoying me with all your yelling.
ZSH
It's grating on me.
BOOM

Meliodas is now dead.
Britannia is ours.
BSSHT
LET'S GO.

Take me there.
But—
Please.

WOOOO
Melio-das... sama ...
An-swer... me.
Melio-das-sama!
HH..
SCUFF

There... you are.
Melio-das-sama...

Please... wake up...
HUG
GRIP
No...
Ah...
Ah...

AAAAAAAHHH!!

Chapter 178 - Britannia in Darkness

ONE MONTH FOLLOWING THE DEFEAT OF THE SEVEN DEADLY SINS' MELIODAS...
...THERE EXISTED PLENTY OF FORCES WHO COULD STAND UP AGAINST THE DEMONS, BUT...

...WERE POWER-LESS IN THE FACE OF THE TEN COM-MAND-MENTS.

THEIR NUMBERS FELL DAY AFTER DAY, AND BRITANNIA'S SPHERE OF INFLUENCE WAS ERODED AWAY BY THE WAVE OF DARKNESS.

FEAR OF THE TEN COMMAND-MENTS THREW A DARK SHADOW OVER THE PEOPLE...
...AS THEY WERE SUBJECTED TO ONE PARTICU-LARLY TER-RIFYING ACT OF THEIRS.
DEMONS FEED ON SOULS.
AND THE TEN COMMANDMENTS FEED ON EXCEPTIONALLY STRONG SOULS.

SOME PEOPLE DID IT TO PROTECT THEMSELVES AND THEIR FAMILIES.
Let's get them!!
OTHERS, BECAUSE THEY WORSHIPPED THE TEN COMMAND-MENTS.
HEE HEE!
We've got them cornered!
Notify him at once!
THEY OFFERED SACRIFICES TO THEM.

TCH!
Hmph... Foolish com-moners! Don't they know who we are?!
Shh! Keep it down!
We're wanted by the kingdom, or did you forget that?!
We are Holy Knights of Liones. The great Ruin and Freesia of the Weird Fangs!
SMACK
YOU IDIOT!
With their Combat Classes...these guys are top quality! The man is at 420...and the chick is 440!
Be careful of their magic powers though!
OOOH!
Har har har!

I won't even have to use my magic against commoners like you!
BASH!
CRUNCH
THNK
SLORSH
I guess now I don't have a choice!
GWAAH!
ZOW
DOOF!
CRAASH
Sac-rifice them!
GHHRK
We must... offer them their souls.
UGH...
Who are these guys?
FZZT
I came once I heard there were some choice picks to be had. Are you the ones?

Ch...
Chief Holy Knight Dreyfus ?!

Ohh... I'd heard that you went missing after the battle in the capital with The Seven Deadly Sins. I never expected to run into you here!
TAP
We were chased out of the capital and not sure what to do next. With you here now, we should be able to gain control over Liones once more. Please let us join you in—

BLOOP
MMPH!
SHOOP
Blemished souls taste awful.
SHLUCK
CHEW
CRUNCH
HE... HE'S DEAD ?!
R... Ruin?
!!
Dreyfus-sama, what did you do to Ruin—?
It's not like you have any people to protect or a country to return to. Accept your death with grace.
LOOM
!!

KAPOW
TCH!!
Fraudrin-sama!
This girl has demonstrated the utmost disrespect toward you!
TAK
HE'S NOT HUMAN!
WAKE UP, YOU DUNG BEETLES!
GRAB
Hey ...!

Of course not, you villainous wench!
He's one of The Ten Commandments!
LET GO! ...KUH!
Let's sacrifice her.
Foolish Human. You would dare defy a Demon?
Knock it off! How can you think of Demons this way?
Have you no pride in your humanity ?!
Pride won't save our families.
Unlike you Holy Knights ...
DAMN YOU ALL! I'LL KILL YOU! YOU MONSTERS !!
I'm willing to bet your soul has more vigor than that other fellow's.
AAH!

Thank you for finding this for me.
As a reward, we'll extend the grace period another three months.
Y-Yes... Thank you, sir!
Fraudrin-sama!
...!

TO THE SLIGHT SOUTH-WEST OF CAMELOT
WAH!
WAH!
WHOOOSH
FLASH

BOOM
DWA-
AAA-
AH!

SLASH
WHOOSH
ZSH

FLASH
CRASH

QUICK DRAW
"MERCILESS CASCADE."
SPLIT

POP
VRRR
STAB
UWAA-ARGH!

SLAM
GRAB
YOU HAVE TWO OPTIONS LEFT. SURRENDER, OR DIE.
YOU DAR OPPOSE US, HUMANS
I choose option number three.
STRAAAIN
THOOM
Wrong

FIGHT YOU TO THE BITTER END!
CLANG

THE SEVEN DEADLY SINS
THOOM
HAH!
FLASH

Chapter 179 - Have Hope

RRRRUMB
KRAAASH

KLASH
I...
HUFF!
HUFF!
I did iiiiit!
HOP
Ooh... Yes!! You certainly did, Arthur-sama!

Still. I never imagine Demon could be so powerf
DIG
Even after taking down one or two of these, I'm still anxious about how things will go after this.
NOM NOM
EITHER WAY, SOME-BODY HAS TO DO IT.
AS LONG AS WE DON'T GIVE UP, SOME DAY THE LIGHT WILL BREAK THROUGH.

King Arthur
That light is none other than you, Arthur-sama.
M... Me? Please!
がばっ
JUMP
It's giving me too much credit to call me the light! If Sir Nanashi weren't here, I would have been toast!
Thank you, Sir Nanashi!

< AS LONG AS THAT CAT CREATURE IS WITH YOU, YOU WILL NOT DIE. >
..?
I wonder what he just said.

VWOOM
VWOO
VWOOM
Uh... Hmmm. Back-to-back battles are a bit much, so...
KING ARTHUR THE DEMONS HAVE SENT REIN-FORCE-MENTS.
POW
POW
KAPOW
RE-TREEEAT!
Kuuuh! We've got to get a lot, lot, lot stronger !!

Meowself, I'd like to see you get stronger too, Arthur.
!!! Y...You can talk?!
Did you talk just now, Cath?!
There's something not right about that cat.
A... And you refer to yourself as "me-owself"?
Don't focus on that, of all things!

FLAP
FLAP

FOREST OF WHITE DREAMS, SOUTH-EAST SIDE

Did you find that Holy Knight ?!
Shit... He got away! The bastard... Just when you think he's vanished, he'll show up somewhere else.
He's probably made it into the Forest of White Dreams by now.
TCH!
There are countless rumors these days of people seeing a crazy monster roaming the forest.
HAAH! HAAH!
ssSHHH
Looks like the fog's thick-ened.
I guess I lucked out.

CLANG
Heh heh heh... Luck. Ha.
It sounds like a joke saying it aloud.
SWAY
HAAH... HAAH...
HAAH!
No matter where I run, every place is crawling with Demons.
A Holy Knight'
staying in this room.
We'd better send word at once.
If we hand over a Holy Knight soul, we'll be saved!

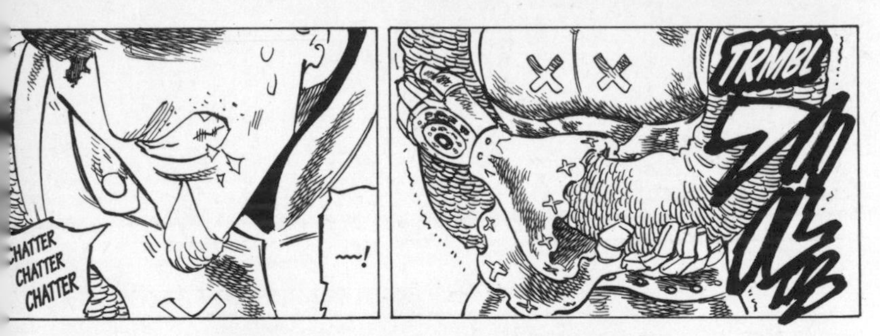
TRMBL
CHATTER CHATTER CHATTER
—!

First I'm defeated by The Seven Deadly Sins and banished from the kingdom...
...and now I'm Demon fodder. What a magnificent turn of events. Heh...heh heh...

BOOOM
Wha ...?!
RATTLE RATTLE RATTLE
TRUDGE
TRUDGE
TRUDGE
That's the sound of foot-steps...
THOOM
A...A Demon?
Ah... Aah... Aaaaaah!

BOOOOOM
WAAA-
AAAH!

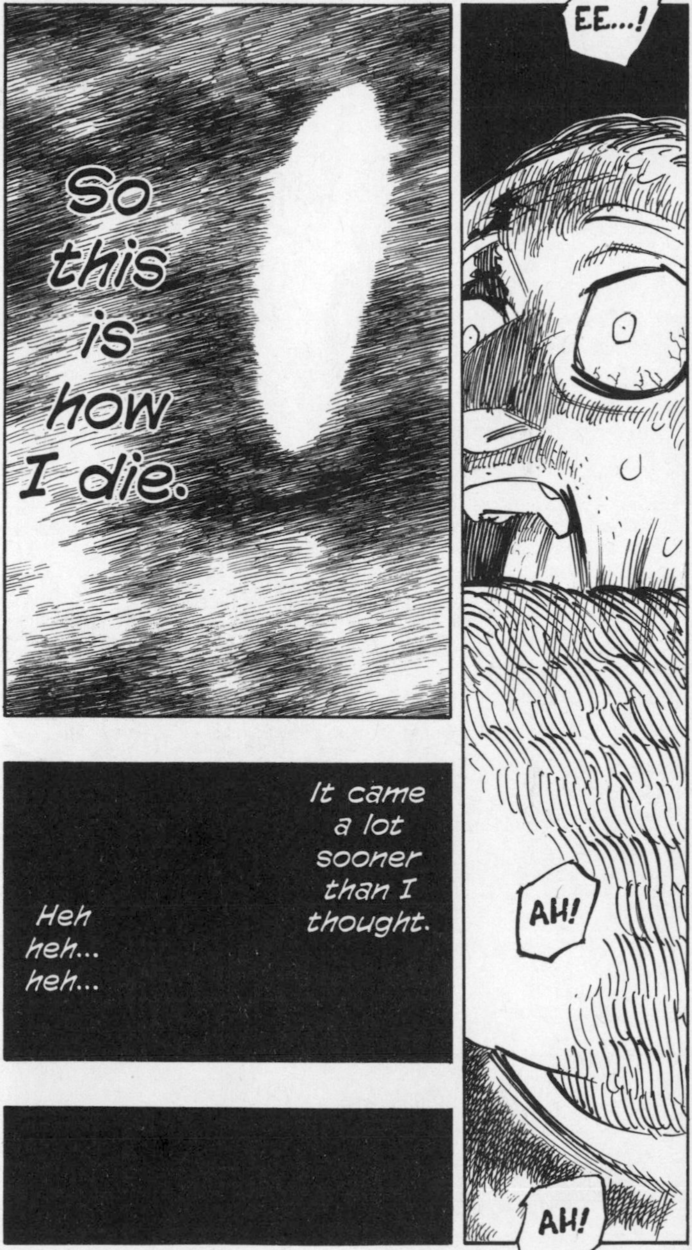

EE...!

So this is how I die.

AH!

It came a lot sooner than I thought.

Heh heh... heh...

AH!

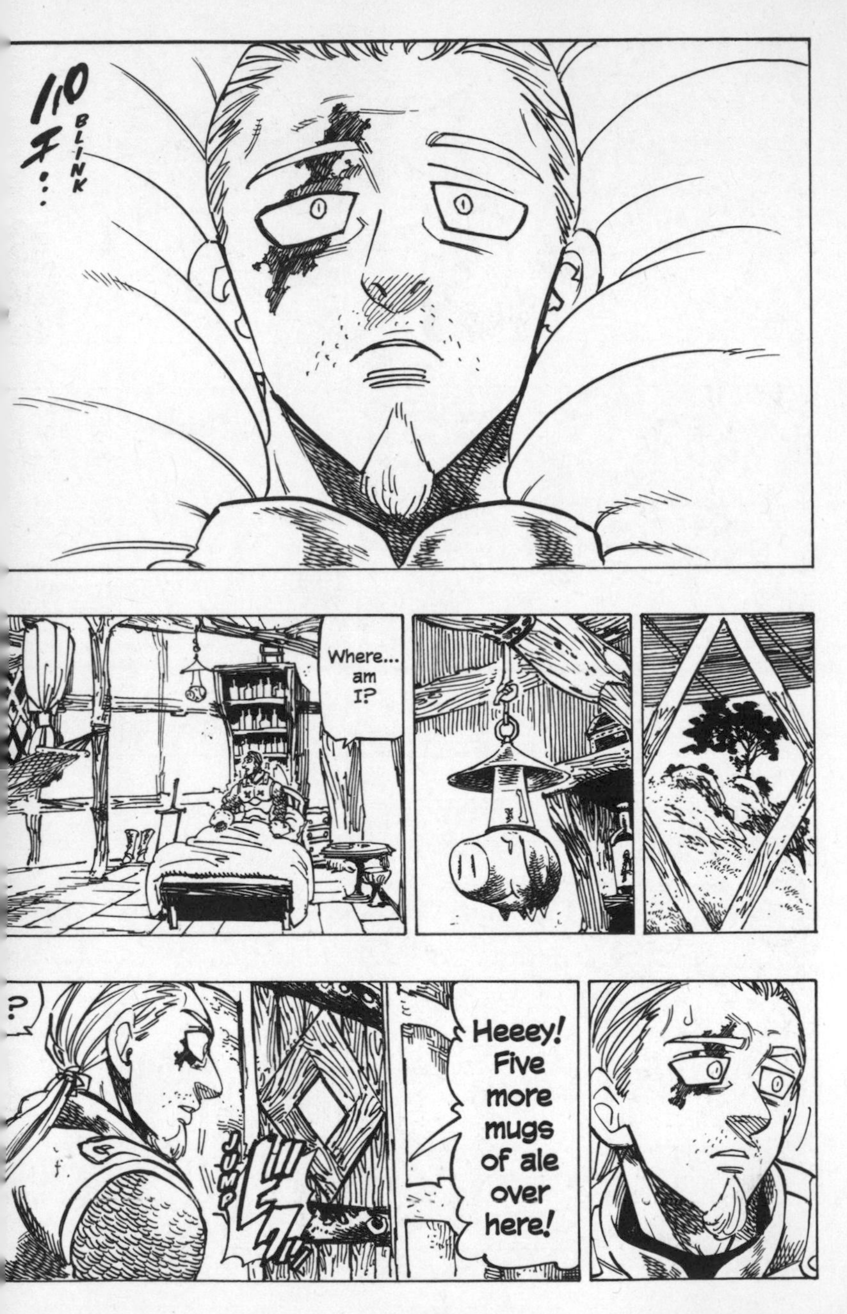
ハチ…
BLINK
Where... am I?
?
JUMP
Heeey! Five more mugs of ale over here!

CHEERS!
HEH HEH!
When I first stumbled upon this pub in the middle of the mountains, I was shocked!
Same here! I thought for sure I'd died and gone to heaven!
...
SIP SIP
It's strange. There wasn't anything here three days ago.
CHUG CHUG
A taver ...?
Thank you for waiting!
Yo! Just what the doctor ordered!
WOOHOO! ♥
Th... That's...

To be continued in Volume 23...

"THE SEVEN DEADLY SINS" ILLUSTRATION CORNER
"THE DRAWING KNIGHTHOOD" SPACE
Be sure to include your name and location with your submission!!
SPECIAL PRIZE
"I'll never give up on anything I set my mind to!!"
"Yeah! That's the spirit, Elizabeth-chan!!"
"Just you watch, Meliodas-sama!!"
The Seven Deadly Sins
AKAYU-SAN / FUKUOKA PREFECTURE
H "Huh? I thought it was me. I'm the mascot of the Boar's Hat! Of The Seven Deadly Sins! Of Britannia itself!!"
MYSTERIOUS K-SAN / AICHI PREFECTURE
ASAMI KAWAMURA-SAN / ISHIKAWA PREFECTURE
D "Sniff...Is he really...really...dead...?"
K "He's not the kind of man... who'd kick the bucket that easily."
M H E D B K G MER Es El J

E "This artist is only five years old and yet she says she like Ban-sama and Elaine! She's wise beyond her years!"
B "Thanks. ♫ I hope you grow up to be a fine young woman. ♫"
MAKO KATOU-SAN / SAITAMA PREFECTURE
K "Now that I think about it, it's odd how these two never age...you know?"
MER "Heh heh... That's because they're both ▇▇."
THE EIGHTH DEADLY SIN-SAN / EHIME PREFECTURE
Es "Such a pity. Without Merlin in the lineup, this game is worthless."
H "Augh! How arrogant!"
KOHARU TAKAMURA-SAN / KANAGAWA PREFECTURE
K "I have to say it. Gowther, don't you think maybe you like dressing like a girl a little too much?"
G "That is because I am so adorable."
七つの大罪
CHOKOMOCHI-SAN / NIIGATA PREFECTURE
H "Let's be happy, everyone!"
K "Yeaaaah! Me too! Me too!!"
J "A-And me too! But first I need a partner!!"
HOSHI-SAN / OSAKA
H "Snoink! Watch me slam dunk this shot!!!"
K "Actually, little Pig... Most of that is thanks to Diane."
HAWK DUNK SHOOT
SUNSUN-SAN / OSAKA

NANA HAMADA-SAN / KOUCHI PREFECTURE
The Seven Deadly Sins
妖精族はキュートなのに めっちゃ強いところが大好きです
"What do you think, Diane? We tried swapping outfits."
"Uwah! ♫ What a scrawny little body! ♫
"I-I didn't ask for your opinion!!"
H "Did you pig jerks hear that?! It says right there I'm number one!!!"
E "Heh heh heh! I'm happy for you!"
B "Yeah, your meat's what's number one, Maste
七つの大罪大好きです
NACHIKA SUZUKI-SAN / NAGANO PREFECTURE
J "Awww, darn it! Are there no better men than Ban out there?!"
H "I'm right here... Can I help you?"
J "Did the piece of ham just say something?"
HAM SANDWICH-SAN / FUKUOKA PREFECTURE

Now Accepting Applicants for the Drawing Knighthood!

- Draw your picture on a postcard, or paper no larger than a postcard, and send it in!
- Don't forget to write your name and location on the back of your picture!
- You can include comments or not. And colored illustrations will still only be displayed in B&W!
- The Drawing Knights whose pictures are particularly noteworthy and run in the print edition will be gifted with a signed, specially-made pencil board!
- The best overall will be granted the special prize of a signed shikishi!!

Send to:
The Seven Deadly Sins Drawing Knighthood
c/o Kodansha Comics
451 Park Ave. South, 7th floor,
New York, NY 10016

- Submitted letters and postcards will be given to the artist. Please be aware that your name, address, and other personal information included will be given as well.

Japan's most powerful spirit medium delves into the ghost world's greatest mysteries!

Story by Kyo Shirodaira, famed author of mystery fiction and creator of *Spiral*, *Blast of Tempest*, and *The Record of a Fallen Vampire*.

Both touched by spirits called yôka Kotoko and Kurô have gained uniqu superhuman powers. But to gain he powers Kotoko has given up an ey and a leg, and Kurô's person life is in shambles. S when Kotoko suggest they team up to de with renegades fro the spirit world, Kur doesn't have many othe choices, but Kotoko might jus have a few ulterior motives...

IN/SPECTRE

STORY BY KYO SHIRODAIRA
ART BY CHASHIBA KATAS

A Kodansha Comics Trade Paperback Original.

Published in the United States by Kodansha Comics, an imprint of Kodansha USA Publishing, LLC, New York.

Publication rights for this English edition arranged through Kodansha Ltd., Tokyo.

First published in Japan in 2016 by Kodansha Ltd., Tokyo.

ISBN 978-1-63236-513-2

Printed in the United States of America.

www.kodanshacomics.com

9 8 7 6 5 4 3 2 1

Translation: Christine Dashiell
Lettering: James Dashiell
Editing: Lauren Scanlan
Kodansha Comics edition cover design: Phil Balsman